Birds

KINGFISHER

Kingfisher Publications Plc
New Penderel House,
283–288 High Holborn,
London WC1V 7HZ
www.kingfisherpub.com

First published by Kingfisher Publications Plc 2003
2 4 6 8 10 9 7 5 3 1
ZIP/0505/PROSP/RNB(RNB)/140MA/F

A CIP catalogue record for this book is
available from the British Library.

ISBN 0-7534-0858-9

Senior editor: Belindà Weber
Designer: Joanne Brown
Picture manager: Cee Weston-Baker
Picture researchers: Joanne Brown, Rachael Swann
Illustrations: Steve Weston
DTP manager: Nicky Studdart
Artwork archivists: Wendy Allison, Jenny Lord
Senior production controller: Nancy Roberts
Indexer: Chris Bernstein

Printed in China

Acknowledgements
The Publisher would like to thank the following for permission to reproduce their material. Every care has been taken to trace
copyright holders. However, if there have been unintentional omissions or failure to trace copyright holders, we apologise and
will, if informed, endeavour to make corrections in any future edition.
b = bottom, *c* = centre, *l* = left, *t* = top, *r* = right

Photographs: cover: Ardea; 6-7 Corbis; 8*b* Corbis; 8-9 Getty Images; 9*b* Nature Picture Library (Nature); 10*t* Getty Images;
10-11 Natural History Picture Agency (NHPA); 11*b* Nature; 12 Bruce Coleman; 13*t* Getty Images; 13*b* Bruce Coleman;
14*b* Corbis; 14-15 NHPA; 15*b* Nature; 16*t* Ardea; 16-17 NHPA; 17*b* Nature; 18 Bruce Coleman; 19*t* Getty Images; 19*c*
Corbis; 19*b* Corbis; 20-21 Still Pictures; 21*c* Ardea; 21*b* Still Pictures; 22-23 Corbis; 23 Nature; 24 Corbis; 25*tl* NHPA; 25*b*
Getty Images; 26*bl* Corbis; 26-27 Corbis; 29 Getty Images; 30 Corbis; 31all Getty Images; 32-33 Getty Images; 33*t*
Nature; 33*b* Getty Images; 36*b* Getty Images; 36-37 National Geographic Images Collection; 37*t* NHPA; 38*b* Corbis; 38*cr*
Bruce Coleman; 39*t* Associated Press; 39*b* Nature; 40 NHPA; 41*t* NHPA; 41*b* Frank Lane Picture Agency; 46*l* Ardea; 46*r*
Corbis; 47*l* Ardea; 47*r*
CorbisCommissioned photography on pages 42–45 by Andy Crawford.
Thank you to models Lewis Manu, Daniel Newton, Lucy Newton, Nikolas Omilana and Olivia Omilana.

 Kingfisher Young Knowledge

Birds

Nicola Davies

Contents

What is a bird?

Birds are everywhere! You can see them in forests, deserts, seas and cities. There are 9,000 different kinds, but every one has wings, a beak, feathers and feet.

Feathers

Birds are the only animals to have feathers. Tail and wing feathers are stiff and strong, while body feathers are silky and soft.

Feet

All birds have scaly feet. They have four toes, for perching or grabbing prey. Eagles have strong talons on their toes.

perching – holding on to something with their feet

Wings

Birds need wings and strong feathers to fly. The bald eagle has large, powerful wings which let it soar and dive fast to catch its prey.

Beak

Birds do not have teeth to bite or chew. They have beaks instead, to grab food whole or peck it into bits. Every bird has the right shaped beak for the kind of food it eats.

prey – *animals eaten by other animals*

Flying made easy

Birds are good at flying because their bodies are made for it. Their bones are hollow and light, and they have big muscles to beat their wings up and down.

Light as a feather

A bird's skeleton weighs less than all its feathers, so it can fly easily.

Safety first

These guillemots have found a safe place to nest high on a cliff top. Flying means they can reach such places, while their predators cannot.

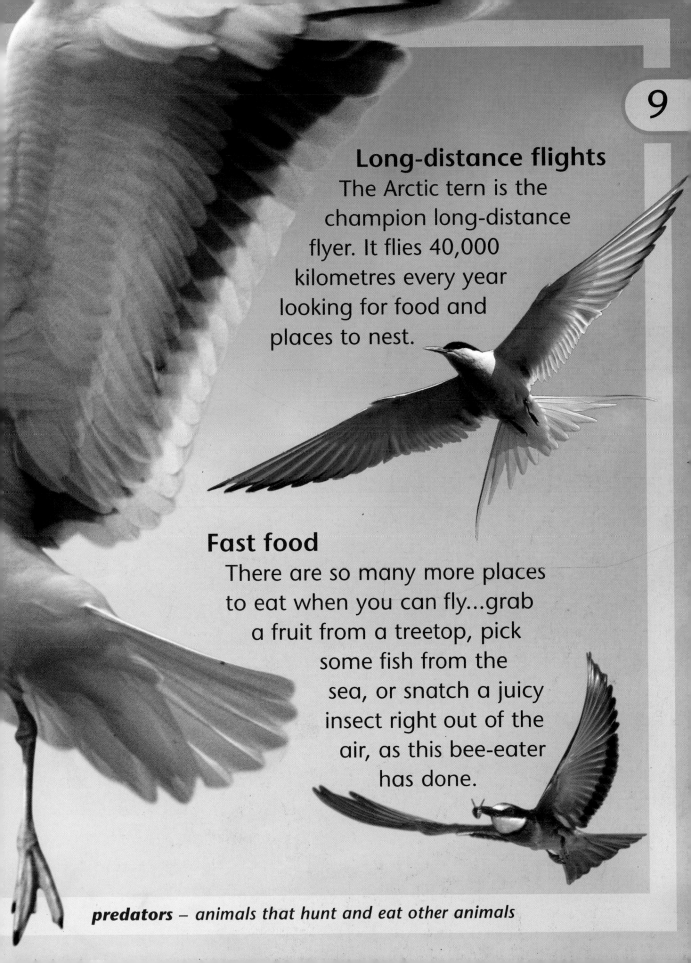

Long-distance flights

The Arctic tern is the champion long-distance flyer. It flies 40,000 kilometres every year looking for food and places to nest.

Fast food

There are so many more places to eat when you can fly...grab a fruit from a treetop, pick some fish from the sea, or snatch a juicy insect right out of the air, as this bee-eater has done.

predators – animals that hunt and eat other animals

Ways of flying

Every kind of bird has a different way of flying, so they all have different shaped wings. Short wings are good for fast flapping and long wings help with gliding.

Up, up...

Taking off is very hard work! This dove has to jump up from the ground or from a perch, then start flapping hard, to get higher and faster.

...and away!

As the dove moves forwards, the air rushing under its wings helps hold it up, so it does not have to flap as hard.

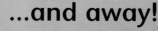

hover – to stay in one place by beating the wings very fast

In a flap
Hummingbirds have short wings that can flap very fast so they can hover in the air.

Hanging around
Vultures have long broad wings that catch the air, so they can glide all day and hardly flap at all.

glide – to fly with wings out, and no flapping

Birds on the ground

Not all birds can fly. Some are too big, some use their wings for swimming instead and some can find food and safety without flying.

Big bird

An ostrich can weigh more than a person. It is too heavy to fly but it can run away from danger at speeds of 72 kilometres an hour.

Flying underwater

Penguin wings are flat and stiff, too small for flight, but they make perfect paddles for diving and swimming underwater.

Look, no wings!

Kiwis, from New Zealand, have no natural predators and feed on the ground. So there is no need to fly and kiwis do not have wings at all!

Hardworking feathers

Birds could not fly without feathers, but feathers do other jobs too. They keep birds warm, hide them from enemies and help them communicate with their friends.

Hiding in summer

It is always hard for predators to find a ptarmigan because in summer it has dark feathers to blend in with summer plants...

communicate – make other animals understand your message

Signal feathers

Macaws have brightly coloured feathers so that they can find each other among the thick leaves of the treetops.

Hiding in winter

...but in winter the ptarmigan stays hidden by growing white feathers to match the snow.

Fantastic feet

blue-footed booby

Birds' feet are made of four long toes, and covered in tough scaly skin. Birds can do a lot more with their feet than just standing, walking or running. They use them for climbing, gripping, swimming, even for saying hello!

Feet for swimming

Many water birds have webbed feet that act as paddles for swimming. The blue-footed booby also waves its brightly coloured feet at its mate to say 'hello'.

webbed feet – feet with skin stretched between their toes

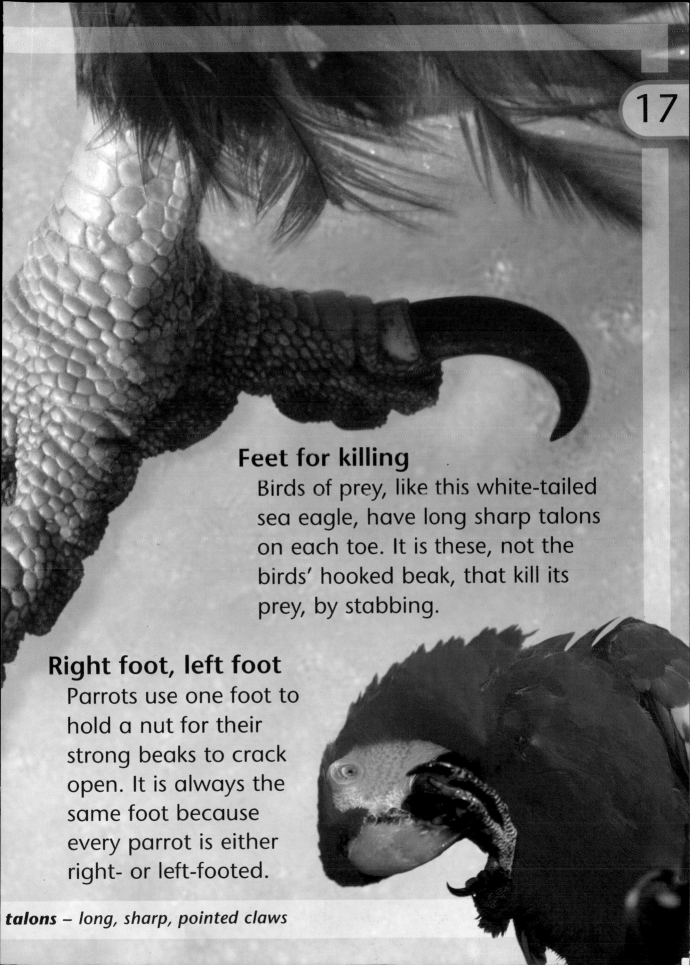

Feet for killing

Birds of prey, like this white-tailed sea eagle, have long sharp talons on each toe. It is these, not the birds' hooked beak, that kill its prey, by stabbing.

Right foot, left foot

Parrots use one foot to hold a nut for their strong beaks to crack open. It is always the same foot because every parrot is either right- or left-footed.

talons – long, sharp, pointed claws

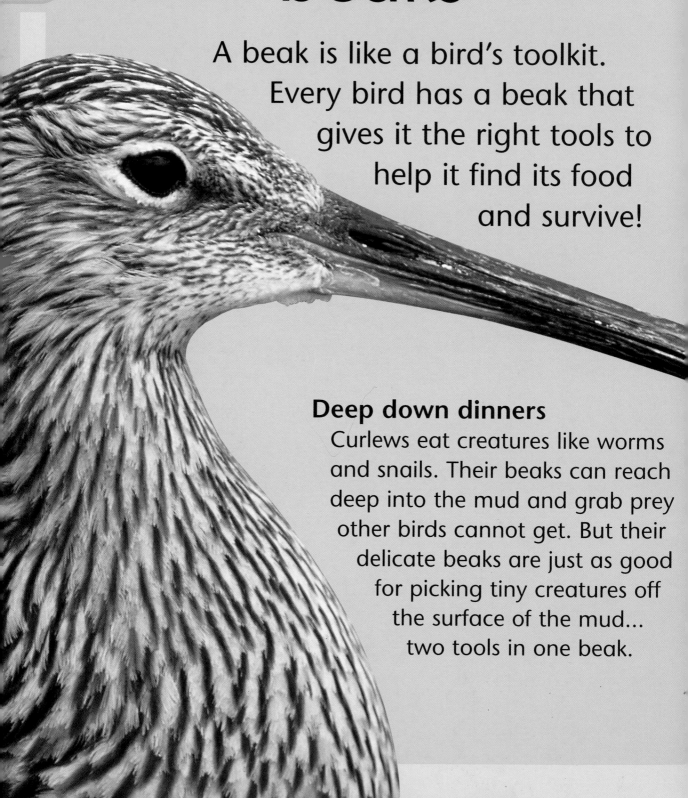

Brilliant **beaks**

A beak is like a bird's toolkit. Every bird has a beak that gives it the right tools to help it find its food and survive!

Deep down dinners

Curlews eat creatures like worms and snails. Their beaks can reach deep into the mud and grab prey other birds cannot get. But their delicate beaks are just as good for picking tiny creatures off the surface of the mud... two tools in one beak.

Fish hooks...and showing off!

Puffin beaks have little spines inside to hold on to slippery fish...and the bright colours send messages to other puffins.

Huge...but not heavy

A toucan's bill is long and bright, but very light because it is hollow.

Tricky tweezers

Pine cones are tough to open. Only a crossbill's beak can do the job, then pick the small, flat, juicy seeds from inside.

bill – another word for beak

Super senses

Birds can use their senses – sight, hearing, touch, taste and smell – to find out about the world around them. But just like humans, their most important senses are sight and hearing.

Invisible ears

Owls' ears are small holes hidden by feathers. But they are so good the owl can find a tiny mouse in the dark, just by sound.

Seeing rainbows

Birds see in colour like we do. These lorikeets eat flowers, so colour helps them to find their food among the green leaves.

I spy, with my little eye

Birds of prey, such as this kestrel, have eyes that can see three times better than humans. They can spot tiny prey on the ground, while they are flying high above.

High-speed hunter

The peregrine falcon is the fastest and most deadly hunter on earth. It can fly at up to 240 kilometres an hour, and its whole body is made for speed and killing.

Tools for the job
Peregrines have super-sharp eyesight for spotting prey, dagger-like talons for grabbing prey, and a hooked beak for tearing flesh into bite-sized pieces.

Stooping for speed...
Peregrine wings are
pointed and narrow for
fast flying but for top
speeds they fold their
wings and dive
down in a 'stoop'.

...and for killing
Stooping is how peregrines
catch nearly all their prey.
They stoop on flying
birds, hitting them with
their talons at more than
160 kilometres an hour.

stooping – when a bird folds its wings and dives through the air

Finding love

When a male bird wants to find a mate, he shows off with a special display. Every kind of bird has a different display. Some birds dance and some birds sing, but they all say the same thing: 'I'm brilliant, be my mate!'

Talking toes

Male blue-footed boobies do not have brightly coloured feathers so they wave their blue feet at the female boobies until one waves back!

display – *when male and female birds 'talk' with special calls and movements*

Brilliant building

The male satin bower bird builds a twig bower and decorates it with blue pebbles, shells and flowers so that a female will notice him. He will even use human litter, as long as it is blue!

Dancing cranes

Male and female cranes get to know each other by dancing, flapping wings and bobbing heads to the sounds of their own calls.

bower – *an arch made of twigs*

Making a home

Birds are fantastic builders!
They make nests of all sizes
and shapes to keep their
eggs and babies safe
from bad weather
and predators.

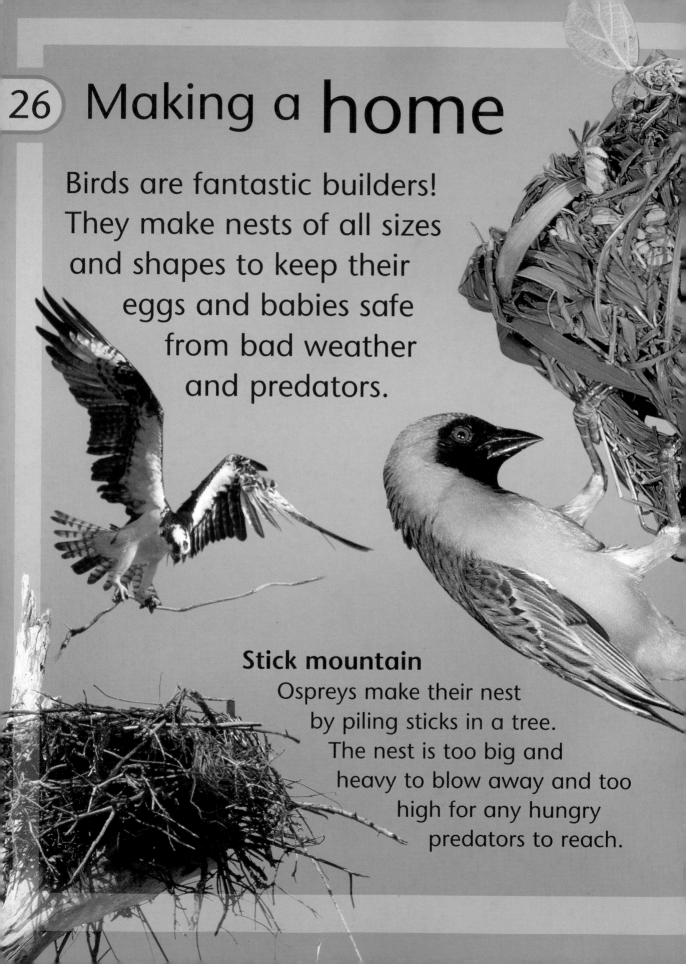

Stick mountain
Ospreys make their nest
by piling sticks in a tree.
The nest is too big and
heavy to blow away and too
high for any hungry
predators to reach.

Hanging around

Weaver birds use grass to weave a ball-shaped nest with one tiny entrance hole. The nest dangles from a twig, so the only way in is by flying.

Tree houses

Hoopoes like hollow trees. They are secure and cosy, and just need lining with grass and leaves to make a nest.

weave – to twist threads and grasses together

Life is egg-shaped!

All birds start life as an egg, laid by their mother. The baby bird grows inside, fed by the yellow yolk and protected by the hard outside shell.

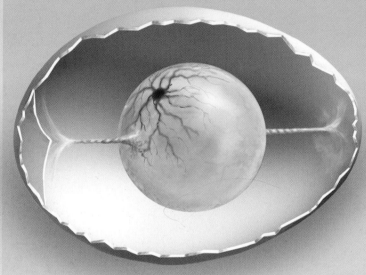

1 A warm start

Inside the egg, the chick starts to grow as soon as incubation begins. It is just a tiny blob, but changes very quickly.

2 Fast food

Food goes straight into the growing chick's tummy from the yolk, and its poo comes out into a little sac.

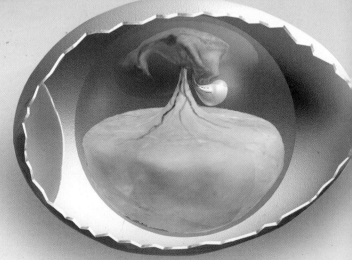

incubation – keeping an egg warm until it hatches

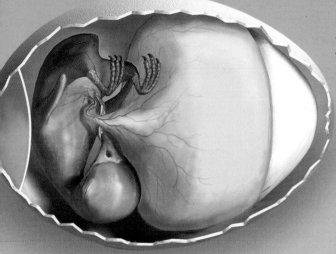

3 Getting into position

As the chick grows and uses up the yolk, it moves to the rounded end of the egg. Its eyes and beak are already formed.

4 Ready for the world

The chick is so big it fills the whole egg! When it is ready to hatch, the chick breaks the air sac and starts to breathe.

Mother hen

As soon as the chick starts breathing, it calls to its mother and she calls back. The birds learn to know each others' voices!

Feathers and fluff

Baby birds do not have proper feathers. Some are covered in fluffy down when they hatch but others are completely naked and grow fluffy feathers later.

Helpless hatchlings

When owlets hatch, they are blind, almost naked and helpless. These have grown their first feathers.

Looking out
This baby chicken's eyes are open, even before it is out of the egg!

Wet-look fluff
It is covered in downy feathers, that are still wet at first...

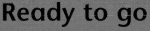

Ready to go
...but they soon dry. In a few hours the chick can leave the nest and follow its mother to look for food.

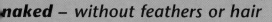

naked – *without feathers or hair*

Bringing up babies

Baby birds are hard work! Bird parents have lots of different ways of giving their babies all the care and food they need.

It takes two...

Both albatross parents have to search hundreds of kilometres of ocean to find enough food for their one chick.

Cheating cuckoos

Cuckoos lay eggs in other birds' nests. The baby cuckoo hatches and pushes the other eggs out. The adult birds raise the cuckoo instead of their babies.

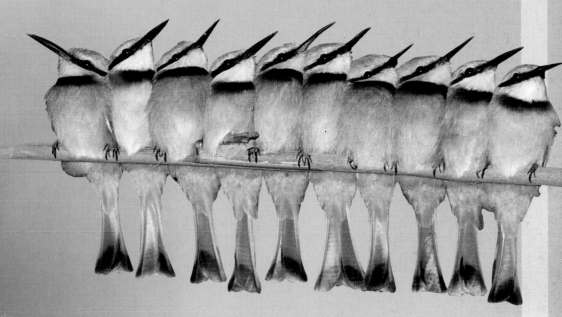

Team work

Mum, dad and a whole team of older brothers and sisters work together to feed the bee-eater babies. The more food they collect, the better chance the babies have of surviving.

Living together

On its own, a bird has just one pair of eyes to look out for danger or for food. But in a flock, there are hundreds of pairs of eyes watching too! The first flamingo to spot trouble raises the alarm and all the flock can fly away.

Party birds

Flamingoes feed and breed together in huge flocks of thousands of birds, that can make whole lakes look pink from far away.

Long-haul
travellers

Every autumn, millions of birds all over the world fly across seas and deserts and mountains to escape from winter, and to find warm weather and food. In the spring, they fly all the way back again!

Finding the way
Geese fly in a 'V' formation. This means they can always see the bird in front which leads the way.

'V' formation – making an arrow pattern

Fat for flying

At migration time, birds get fat to give them the energy they need for their journey.

Safety in numbers

Birds gather together before migration, and travel in large flocks. This means they all leave at the right time and no-one gets lost!

migration – making the same journey every year at the same season

Birds in danger

People are bad news for birds. Hundreds of birds are in danger of becoming extinct because of what we have done. But it is not too late to make things better.

Pet parrots

Wild parrots are sometimes sold as pets. We can stop this by never buying birds that have been taken from the wild.

Bathing birds

Oil spills kill millions of sea birds. Many birds can be saved by washing them clean, and keeping them safe and warm until their feathers have dried.

extinct – none left alive anywhere on earth

Condors going up!

Rare Californian condors nearly became extinct. In 1987, there were only 22 Californian condors left in the world. Then they were bred in zoos, and put back in the wild. Now there are almost 200!

Losing their homes

The forests where the Philippine eagles live are being cut down. But local people are learning how to protect the birds and their forest homes.

The secret life of birds

There are lots of things we do not know about birds. Scientists have developed different ways of finding out more about their mysterious lives.

Penguin radio

The radio tag on this Adelie penguin's back sends out a signal that tells scientists how far it travels and how deep it dives to find its food.

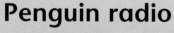

radio tag – a device that sends out invisble signals that travel long distances

Give me a ring!

The ring being put on this bird's leg carries a unique number, so the bird can be tracked all its life, to find out how long it lives.

Who's who?

Coloured rings on this rare wrybill's legs help us tell it apart from other wrybills. Scientists can work out how many there are left and find ways to help protect them.

unique – the only one

42 Make a bird book

Make your own bird scrapbook

It is fun to keep a scrapbook about all the different types of bird you see. You can note down what they look like, where you saw them and what time of year it was. All these things will help you to understand birds better.

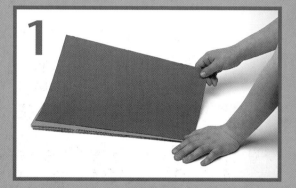

Collect some sheets of different coloured plain paper. If necessary, trim the pages so that they are all about the same size.

You will need
- Coloured paper
- Hole punch
- Ribbon or string
- Sweet wrappers
- Feathers
- Sequins
- Wrapping paper
- Orange peel
- Scissors
- Paint brush
- Glue

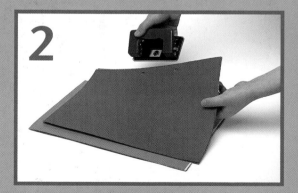

Taking care to keep your fingers out of the way, punch holes in the pages of your book. Make sure that all the holes line up.

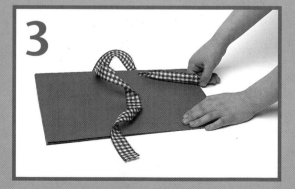

Thread some brightly coloured ribbon or string through all the pages, to keep them together. Leave the ends at the front.

Tie the ends of the ribbon together in a loose bow. This will mean that the pages turn more easily, without ripping.

Draw a picture of a bird on the front of your book. Think about the different colours and textures of the materials you have gathered and make a collage. The beak is hard, so card or plastic will be good. Birds' feet are scaly, so dried orange peel or sequins will give the right texture.

Collect feathers and sweet wrappers to decorate the front of your book. Dried orange peel adds texture.

44 Feed the birds

Make a bird table

Birds make welcome visitors to any home. Encourage local birds to dine at this easy-to-make bird table

Very carefully, cut the sides out of a clean, empty ice cream carton. Leave wide 'legs' of plastic at each corner.

You will need
- Ice cream carton
- Scissors
- Moulding dough
- Compass
- String
- Bird seed

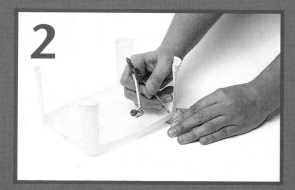

Using a compass, make a hole near the top and the base of each leg. Use a lump of moulding dough to protect your hands.

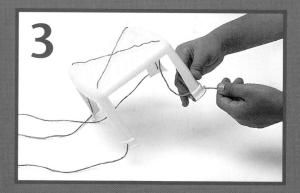

Thread the string through the holes making a cross on the bottom and leaving long ends. You can tie the ends over a branch to hang your table. Put in plenty of bird seed and watch for visitors.

Seed cake treat

Every bird has its favourite food, but this bird cake is a treat many will enjoy.

You will need

- Plastic cup
- String or wire
- Scissors
- Moulding dough
- Saucepan
- Wooden spoon
- Lard or solid fat
- Bird seed

1 Make a hole in the bottom of a plastic cup, protecting your hands with a ball of moulding dough. Thread the string or wire through.

2 Tie a knot in the end at the bottom of the cup. Leave the other end long, so you can hang your seed cake out for the birds.

3 Ask an adult to melt some fat in a saucepan, then carefully stir in the seeds. Fill the cup with the mixture, keeping the string free.

4 Once the cake has set, carefully cut away the cup. Now you can hang the cake outside for the birds to feast on.

Using nestboxes

Different homes for different birds

Each kind of bird has its favourite place to nest. So when you put up a nestbox, make sure it is the right shape and size, and in the right place, for the birds in your area.

Ducks in trees

Black-bellied whistling ducks like to nest in holes in trees. Boxes, attached to tree trunks, are just as good!

Pretend it is a hole

Many small birds, like tits, nest in tree holes. A box with a small entrance to keep out predators seems just like a treehole to a tit.

Up on the roof

Storks like to nest in high trees or on rooftops, but a special platform like this above the roof of a house is even better!

Treetop owls

Barn owls want to feel safe, high up in an old barn, or in a treehole. So this big nestbox five metres up a wall is safe and sound.

Making the birds welcome

- Choose the right box for the birds you want to attract
- Make sure it is firmly attached to a tree or wall
- Check the fittings each year and replace any damaged parts
- If you have to visit the box, do so quietly
- Do not re-visit your nestbox once a family has adopted it
- Remove old nests at the end of each season

Index